Praise for **Paradise and Other Lost Places**

"I couldn't stop reading. Miller takes us on a journey of beauty, grace, and the slow fire of reality burning all around us. His deep observational voice calls us into wandering, silence, and discovery. Stunning, gut-wrenching, and spellbinding, *Paradise and Other Lost Places*, reminds us what it means to be lost, to be found again, to be human."

—Chris Baron, *The Gray*

PARADISE
and Other Lost Places

PARADISE
and Other Lost Places

jim miller

SD
CWP
SAN DIEGO
CITY WORKS
PRESS

ISBN: 978-0-9837837-7-0
Library of Congress Control Number: 2024941564

San Diego City Works Press is a non-profit press, funded by local writers and friends of the arts, committed to the publication of fiction, poetry, creative nonfiction, and art by members of the San Diego City College community and the community at large. For more about San Diego City Works Press please visit our website at www.cityworkspress.org.

San Diego City Works Press is extremely indebted to the American Federation of Teachers, Local 1931, without whose generous contribution and commitment to the arts this book would not be possible.

Cover design: Perry Vasquez
Production editor: Will Dalrymple

Published in the United States by San Diego City Works Press, California
Printed in Canada

For Walter and Kelly

contents

Paradise Lost

This Is It

This Much I Know About Desire

PIONEER INN

Paradise Lost

At the Pioneer Inn, Lahaina, Maui

Before falling asleep,
I gaze at the cheap painting
of the Pioneer Inn
on the wall of my room there—
a rendering of the old hotel
from just offshore,
perhaps from the deck of a small craft
docked in the harbor.
Moonlight glitters on the water
and the cabins of the boats
tied up by the shore
are aglow from within
as is the inn itself.
Its rustic bar is in the forefront
with the side of the building
adorned with
elegant white lanais
bounded by palms.
Across the street
the huge banyan tree looms over the park
and the mountains in the distance
are crowned by scattered white clouds
illuminated by a waxing moon.
Bathed in blue light, the scene
is a window into a dream.

The morning after,
I sat on the lanai
and thought of Mark Twain's visit here,
when the aspiring young artist
marveled at the beauty
of the island
and satirized the American missionaries
who could never really see it,

hunkered down in their spare white churches,
set on bringing tales of hell to paradise.

Of his time on Maui, Twain wrote that he "went to stay a week
and remained five," wistfully noting how he
"never spent so pleasant a month before, or bade
anyplace goodbye so regretfully."
With no care for "business or human toil or sorrow or weariness"
he dove into the heart of the gorgeous now.

Even early on this summer morning,
the crowd is building, swarming the streets.
I turn and look in the other direction
at the vast, deep blue Pacific,
vivid and endangered,
at risk of being exploited,
and loved to death
by those who Twain called "the damned human race."
But there it is, nonetheless, glistening,
beckoning me to surrender to
wonder.

Fire Song

Dreaming of fire raging,
I wake sweating
in the humid dark
of a strange hotel room,
listen to the ceiling fan squeak
and turn on my side
to gaze out the window
at the empty street.
Always a war within,
always fear,
always desire.

That morning
I drive to the edge of town
past the tourist stores
and a big blue sign
that says
"JESUS COMING SOON."

At the Jodo Mission
I stroll through the grounds
admiring the symmetry
of the lush green gardens,
and stare up at the
Buddha sitting
in full lotus,
surrounded by offerings
of mangos, bananas,
and rich, scarlet plumerias.
His face is serene
against the background
of the ancient volcano.

Across the street
by the beach,
in Puupiha cemetery,
I see pillows and blankets
next to a grave,
melted candles
and children's toys
left for the dead.
Some of the markers
are marble blocks
with intricate characters,
others are just
oblong stones
that one might find anywhere.

How brilliant the azure sea,
I think to myself—
Just see the blueness
of blue,
the man catching a fish,
the dog drinking water
from a can of dried-out flowers.
These are the things
that will teach you
to live.

Earth Song

I awoke
in a strange room
surrounded by
the heart of the night,
and heard groans of love
through the wall
like the moans
of dying.

Then I laid there,
restlessly,
half asleep,
with a strange,
unsettling reverie that
traveled with me—
digging a hole
in jet black earth
that got deeper and deeper
until closing over,
enfolding me gently in
a womb of pure darkness.

That morning,
at the hotel bar,
I drank coffee
while the heat built,
paid my bill
and took a stroll
down the street.
By an old church
I found a graveyard
and sat for awhile
near the tomb of a child.

What would you have thought
of the late morning light?
Of the song of the birds?
Of the hunger for more
than the moment can yield?
And would you have dreamed
of the embrace of the earth,
you who know it so well?

After the Fire

I saw it on TV—
the Jodo Mission in Lahaina
lies in ruins,
devoured by fire,
the temple, the meeting house, the house
where a family lived,
destroyed.

Founded in 1912 by Japanese immigrants
who labored in the cane fields and
the pineapple plantations
along with Chinese, Portuguese, and Filipino workers
who came to form the heart
of the CIO in the Thirties,
bringing the promise of
dignity and democracy
to those on whose backs
Hawaii was built.
In 1937, union workers held the first May Day parade on Maui,
thousands of them marching,
complete with an eight-piece band
and banners that read,
"Make this a workers' paradise."

The Mission served as a community hub
for years to come
until, in 1968,
a fire took the original buildings.
It was then that the 12-foot Amida Buddha statue
was sent from Kyoto, Japan,
in honor of the immigrant ancestors
who were the first Japanese to come to Maui.
And it stood there,
majestically framed by

the mountains behind it,
for over five decades.

Now, the Buddha sits in lonely vigil
amidst the desolation
on Puunoa point,
in sight of Lanai and Moloka'i
inviting your gaze to the distant horizon.

Never forget the transient nature of all things,
the Buddha's solitary witness reminds us,
but also know that
we are always becoming,
like the newly formed shoots
on the scorched banyan tree
down the road.

No matter how hard the path,
in one form or another,
we persist.

News From the World

At dawn, just after
the first rooster crowed,
we got up and walked to the beach,
crossed the lawn
to the sandy path,
strewn with lava rocks,
made our way toward the boat launch,
and almost stumbled upon
a green turtle,
sleeping like a drunk
with his head flopped out in front of him,
and his flippers splayed by his sides as
the water slowly rippled up to kiss him.
When he heard us
he opened one eye, lazily,
so we stepped back several feet,
quietly,
savoring our good fortune,
grateful for this gift
of amazement
at first light.
Then just as we came upon him
we left him in peace to slumber
a bit longer before he
slid back into the welcoming arms of the sea.

How can you not love a world with such creatures in it?

In the brush by the shore,
Another rooster crowed
and a flock of chicks
scurried across the black rocks, cheeping.

A gentle breeze began to stir,
and the surf started its serenade,
reminding us
of the simple joy
of being alive.

Later that evening
I saw it on the news on TV—
New York City was choking on smoke
from burning forests in Canada.
The wildfires were scorching acre after acre
of pristine wilderness
that will not recover
in our lifetimes,
if ever.

The world is burning faster and more furiously
than even our love can repair.

On the Waihee Ridge Trail

Coming down from above the clouds
on the Waihee Ridge Trail
with mist drifting languidly
over the treetops,
they were singing together,
hidden somewhere in the brush.
I stopped in my tracks
to search the landscape for the birds.
Seeing none, I gave up
and continued on,
one step after the other
carefully navigating the
steep, muddy decline of the path,
hopping over rocks
and large divots along the way.
Keeping my eyes down,
I noticed the viscous mud
caked on my shoes,
wiped sweat from my forehead.
Lost in the rhythm of the hike,
I am awakened by a burst of song,
look up and see three birds,
with intense red and black markings,
dart from a bare tree branch on the hillside
into the heart of the verdant foliage
that covers the uneven terrain
on the side of the ridge that overlooks
the river
in the valley below.
I stop and marvel at the apparition
of these rare Hawaiian honey creepers,
perhaps destined for extinction,
passing through this moment in time,

and blessing me with a
tragic awe.

Pirates

Having escaped the blaring heat
of the beach for the day
I sit in the shade of a palm tree
by the shore,
to read a book about pirates.
In the midst of many tales of travail,
blood, suffering, and death,
I am struck by the story of an ancient buccaneer,
captured and brought
before Alexander the Great
who asked him,
"What he meant by keeping hostile possession
of the sea?"
Undaunted, the scofflaw replied that
his motivation was similar to Alexander's
in "seizing the whole earth."
"But because I do it with a petty ship," the pirate went on,
"I am called a robber
whilst thou who do it with a great fleet
art styled emperor."

I stopped with the book in my lap
and smiled, thinking of how
the lords of our realm
have plundered the planet,
despoiled the earth,
colonized our minds,
and locked us in a prison of measured time,
leaving us no other option but
to steal our precious minutes back again—
like the contraband sight of
the golden road of sunlight gently glowing
on the water
as dolphins jump

and play on the horizon.
This and the simple pilfering of
one breath after another,
taken with no purpose,
or the capture of
the serene sound
of the surf,
and the free smell of the
salty,
bracing,
sea air.

The Day After Father's Day

The morning glow
brightens the screw pines
while the joyous racket
of birds
welcomes the new day.
I watch a butterfly
glide aimlessly
over sunlit green leaves
as a dragonfly hovers
steadily nearby
holding onto its stillness
despite the furious movement of its wings.
A mynah struts across the lawn,
a worm dangling in its beak,
against the backdrop of white flowers
undulating in the breeze
as the gorgeous Pacific glints
through the open spaces in the hedge
by the rocky driveway.

Today, we will stroll to the red sand beach
before the crowds arrive,
hike across the lava rocks by the sea,
and walk the steep path
to the top of the hill
and stand by the cross
surveying the whole landscape—
the herds of cattle
on the luxuriant green hillsides,
the stark white churches,
and the battered pier on the bay.
Tucked in the midst of it all is the
quaint ballpark
with a black sand infield,

where the San Francisco Giants once
spent spring training,
and my son and I will play catch
when it's empty,
filled with pure joy
as the sound of the ball popping
in our gloves
ushers in the bittersweet
twilight.

Our Lady of Fatima Shrine, Wailua, Maui

It's not the pious simplicity
of the spare white chapel
that moves me
but the greenness of
the taro field beside it,
the anarchic banana patch
behind the cemetery,
the impropriety of the impatiens,
magenta, purple, and pink
between gravestones,
and the crawling vines
reaching up to the cross
to pull a suffering Christ
down to moist black earth.

Swimming

I am silent in
the presence of
the blue depth
of the ocean,
silent in the face
of the immensity
of sky and
the mystery of stones,
not to mention the
incredible puzzle of
hidden sea,
a myriad of strange creatures
and improbable life.

The physicists tell us
that the whole of the universe
is a fluid event,
a miraculous Shiva's dance
of matter,
veiled to the naked eye,
that joins us with everything
in the flux of becoming.

I think of this,
swimming past waves
to the deep water,
that somehow
I am the ocean,
the sky,
the stones,
and the fish—
big as it all
and at the same time
nothing.

Then suddenly
I'm in too deep,
past the point
where the bottom is visible
and with the chill
of the current
I tremble,
turn back,
and swim to
the shore.

On the beach
I pant
and feel the air
deep in my lungs,
the sun on my back,
and the sand hot underfoot.
I sit for a moment
to rest as
the breeze blows
my skin dry.

There are too many things
to do today
that just don't matter.

I see again
the imperturbable ocean,
rising with wind,
washing away stone.

The Ruins Near Hana

Here by the ruins
I nurse the abundance of the deep green jungle
and the native fruit trees and flora thriving by
the cerulean sea.
It is the kind of beauty that
brings tears
and makes you muse about the
elusive nature of human happiness
in a world full of such radiance.
But then I come back to myself
and remember how many people died here,
laid waste by murder and disease.
All so we could bring them a new God
and the wonders of Western commerce
that would steal their land,
rape their culture, and make it possible
for me to sit in a lounge chair on a perfect day
by the Pacific and read these lines by
Leonard Cohen: "We are meant for chains
tho every atom's free
and even beauty meets an edge
As one can plainly see."

In Makawao

At the street fair
in Makawao
I found grace
somewhere in the
intensity of dusk.
Walking down the main drag
with the anarchic green foliage
teeming just past
the rooftops
of the bakery, coffee shop,
and dress stores,
mingling with paniolos
and old hippies,
surveying the food trucks, rodeo posters,
and handmade jewelry.
At the main stage,
The Haiku Hillbillies
played "Deep Elem Blues"
and fell into a long jam—
the guitar, banjo, and violin
merging sweetly as the sky
turned ruby red above the town.
Two young girls skipped into
the center of the action,
swinging arm in arm
beside an elderly Japanese couple
stepping slowly in tender embrace
and a winsome young mother
in a flowing paisley skirt
bouncing her baby
to the music
and gleefully holding the
giggling child aloft
to the wide grins

of passersby.
Something about it all captured me
as I leaned against a fence post, smiling.
The Hillbillies moved into a
song about the road to Hana where
the switchback turns and dense jungle
force you to "search and find."
I looked up at the last few moments of
the burning heavens
finally feeling
beyond despair
while the joy arose in me
and the world within and without
was dancing, ecstatic,
transcendent
as the last light
bled into the night sky.

The Red Hens in the Labyrinth

So much can be learned
by taking a walk in the labyrinth
in a sacred garden
as the cool breeze ripples though
the surrounding forest
and you place one foot
in front of the other
painstakingly trying to count
the number of steps that coincide with
each in-breath and then
with each out-breath.
You feel the ground under your feet,
listen to the birds
concealed in the trees around you,
hold your balance with discipline
so you stay within the lines.
Despite the awkward process,
there is an elegance to it,
you think as you reach
the center,
only to be greeted by a flock of red hens
who break all the rules
as they rush across the circle of lines,
brush past your legs,
and peck at your toes
for good measure.

On the lawn by the greenhouse,
a rooster crows loudly,
his feathers puffed out dramatically,
before chasing off a rival
and strutting back
to occupy the main stage.
But the hens don't care.

They just sally forth
from the inner circle
and make their way to the forest
where they dig their claws
into the fresh earth
as if nothing had happened
other than what
always is.

In the Jungle Towns

After genocide, syphilis,
disenfranchisement, economic ruin
and a tourist invasion
the Hawaiians in the jungle towns
sit in their gardens
and watch rental cars roll by
to snap pictures of
timeworn sand and coral churches,
sandwiched between rainforest
and raging blue sea.
The missionaries came
to do good
and they did quite well
but what's holy
isn't the Puritan dream—
it's the blood of the dead,
the names of animals
no one remembers,
hard calluses on the hands
of the men in the cane fields,
the kind-faced women
at roadside stands,
and the fact that the service
is slow.

Learning to Be No One

A desire to be inside the inexhaustibility.
—Karl Ove Knausgaard, *My Struggle*

1

Alone on the plane I had the same thought that I always do—"we could crash and my life might end at any time." Images of the moments before death subsumed me. I imagined the faces of my fellow passengers contorted in horror. I heard the weeping, the screaming, the voices futilely attempting to leave last messages to their loved ones on their cellphones, all to no avail.

My fantasy was real enough that amidst a banal announcement about expected turbulence, I came close to tears as I thought of never seeing my wife or son again and went on to consider the weight of the collective losses of all the souls on the plane.

But, in this case, what used to be a source of physical anxiety gave way to a feeling of absolute groundlessness.

There is something liberating about anonymity and the small pleasure of being unrecognized in the odd womblike environment of a passenger jet. You can, for what it's worth, escape yourself and all the baggage that comes with the identity you have handed to you in your official "life" however briefly.

But with this lack of recognition comes the reality that you are no one to everyone there. And you have no connection to the other souls all around you other than your shared role as paid passengers, who will surely receive what Melville called "the universal thump" despite your privileged status as the recipients of free snacks delivered to you by the harried flight attendants as they manically push the cart up and down the aisle dishing out drinks and hermetically-sealed treats or boxed breakfasts and then reverse course to collect trash before coming back with yet another generic item for your consumption.

I was struck by the utter meaninglessness of the ritual that was well beyond alienation. It was life emptied out and performed over and over again, in a purgatorial fashion. I wanted to squirm out of my skin, jump out the emergency door, but I just sat there forgetting why anything I had ever done mattered, why anything mattered, for that matter.

It was all a nothing we know too well despite our protestations.

Indeed, for a moment in time somewhere above the Pacific Ocean, my identity shattered and was taken over by something else, so much so that that thing which I call "me" was close to disappearing entirely.

It was a sense that I could very well lose control of everything. And this feeling went to the root of me in a way that might have evoked terror or despair but, during this instance, I was simply aware of an unraveling. I became my dissolution and sat in my cramped seat next to the businessman on his laptop and the nondescript woman sleeping under her shawl, becoming no one.

"What is this?" I asked myself. What is this thing I call myself?

I held close to the heart of that quivering instant and rode with it, feeling the contours of this strange state of being while I observed people on their devices, playing games, watching movies, distracting themselves with whatever they could amidst the low hum of the jet engines. All the while I was there but not there, inside and outside of myself at the same time.

I thought about the space of an hour detached from place, floating in the air, felt time randomly slow down and speed up as if on a whim.

My thought was: "I am a man sitting on a plane unsuccessfully trying to read a book by an author from Norway while eating a packaged meal and occasionally looking out the window at the pale blue sky."

As I held tightly to an image of myself as a man on a plane going somewhere, the sense of disintegration eased, and I came back to a feeling of solidity and the idea that I was someone who reads novels on airplanes and thinks too much.

I got up and peed in the claustrophobic bathroom and washed my hands carefully while avoiding the reflection of my face in the mirror. On the way back to my seat, I looked at the bland visages of my fellow passengers and took some comfort in the thought that all of us were lost between time zones, hurtling through space toward a given destination.

We would again be someplace soon.

2

At the airport in Kahului, the first thing that strikes you is the dense soft air. Here I am in the luxurious breeze—getting my bags, waiting for the shuttle, making small talk with the driver, a sweet Hawaiian woman from the Big Island. Each small thing is a pleasure now that you are out of the air, time is slower, and the world is full of promise again.

After I got my cheap rental car at a place with a herd of cats in the office, I drove a few blocks down the main drag in Kihei by some Seventies-style ranch houses where the locals live on one side and tourist condos are on the other. I stopped to buy groceries in a supermarket that could have been anywhere but for the small touches of Maui in the forms of boogie boards for sale by the checkout, a poke counter, and piles of mangoes, papayas, and apple bananas.

The cashiers say "Aloha" and "Mahalo."

I loaded my car full of groceries in the parking lot and listened to the mynah birds screeching in the tree by my parking space. A woman and her son were tying a mattress to the roof of their van next to me with a flimsy string. I excused myself as I opened the driver's side door and said, "You'll have more room now," before I backed out and rolled through the parking lot back to the street.

When you drive on Maui it's important that you slow-the-fuck down. It's considered rude to not let people get in front of you and it's even worse to tailgate. In other words, a key to settling into the local culture, to not being seen as an asshole from the mainland, is to stop being one.

Thus, I slowed-the-fuck down, waved people on in front of me, found the island music station on the radio with its charmingly sentimental Hawaiian reggae, and let the radiance of the day, the brilliant sun, the sea by the main drag, the locals hanging by food trucks in the park, sink in seamlessly.

It was as easy as taking your clothes off.

3

When I got to the timeshare, I unpacked, stocked the place with groceries, changed into my shorts, and took a jog by the glittering ocean, feeling the sea air and hot sun on my body as I plodded and panted down the beach, one bare foot after the other struggling through the sand.

These simple tasks seem to ground me somehow. Later, as I sat on the lanai reading the same book of Norwegian fiction, listening to early Bob Marley on the stereo, and staring out at the endless horizon of the sea, I was overcome with a feeling of boundlessness.

The shattered feeling on the plane returned and was transformed into a kind of ecstatic joy.

As I lost myself in the landscape painting of the emerging sunset, the waves on the lava rocks below my balcony was the song of the world, the sound of the planet breathing and me breathing along with it.

I was inside of everything and yet outside of it at the same time.

When the music on the stereo stopped, I closed my eyes for a while and just listened to the cadence of the surf, lilting. When I opened my eyes again the golden light was so blinding that it hurt to hold my gaze but I squinted hard and bore with it. And after the burning sun dropped below the horizon, I drank in the blood red sky and nursed the subtle changes that each moment brought as the clouds danced with the dying light.

There is no describing the vast love that wells up in you when you find yourself in rapture with the stunning, naked radiance of the world.

The redness of red.

To be present and alone with the resonance of everyday life annihilates us.

The borderland of twilight.

We long for places we'll never be able to go but still desire nonetheless.

The deep well of grief that gives birth to joy.

"This is why we are alive," I thought.

I was mad to be in contact with it, whatever it was.

The Deer on Lanai

After swimming in the crystalline sea
we surveyed the tide pools by the beach,
basking in the bounty of starfish, urchins,
triggerfish, parrot fish, squirrel fish,
Moorish idols, and more.
The small ones sought refuge in the shallows
before venturing into the dangers
of the waters beyond.

On the walk
back to the ferry,
a herd of deer rushed across
the road in front of us
to the shade of the trees by the shore,
their graceful, elegant movements
like a cool glass of water
on a scorching hot day.

They are out of place here,
brought
to serve as game
but, instead, they thrived while
slowly killing off native plants,
yet another bit of human folly
that has come back to curse the islands.

Nonetheless, they are adorable,
and I can't help but love them
as they stare at us
with their big moist eyes—
beautiful and innocent.

After our boat left the harbor
it hugged the coast for a while,

just long enough for
a pod of dolphins to emerge,
a marvelous surprise
by the side of the ferry.
As the winds picked up
on the way back to Maui,
I glanced out toward the deep ocean
past the islands,
and held my hat to my head
while the cold spray hit my face
and the boat began to pound against
the oncoming waves.

How many precious things
will be lost
in just this one lifetime?

Kilauea Lodge, Volcano, Hawaii

The chorus of their calls
echoed magically
in the darkness.
And if you listened deeply,
you noticed an odd "koo-kee"
out of step with the collective chorus.

These invasive frogs
are unwelcome here,
but still play a part
in the melody
like a dissonant jazz riff.

Then, underneath that, buried
in the deep texture of sound
the humming of insects
began to keep pace,
sometimes interrupted by the
unexpected trill of a stray bird.

The immaculate harmony
at the heart of the chaotic music
is all that I'll ever need
in this short,
yet beloved life.

Molokai

With my hand on her belly
as she tosses and turns,
struggling with the new life
within her—one tiny speck of big being—
like the barely discernable light
of a single star
lost in the immensity of night sky.
The sound of the ocean lull
in the near distance
does not bring me sleep.
Instead, I think of the infant's grave
outside the spare white chapel
by the seaside
and the priest's words on the sign
at the cusp of the cliff overlooking
the colony where so many died—
"One's Molokai can be anywhere."
Some of the lepers were cast off ships
into shark-filled waters,
others rudely abandoned
on the barren black lava.

How cruel the azure blue Pacific,
how mean the dense, shaded green of the tumid shore.

I stare at nothing
unable to yield
as I listen to the ceiling fan whirl
frantically
and think
"We crucify each other."

She moans in her sleep
and rolls over.

Before dawn comes the birds' song
and I lose myself
as she and I
and the world
keep breathing.

This Is It

This Is It

Her naked body
and the anonymous
space of the motel
bed were made
holy by it,
that one true second when
the bottle of whiskey was
like the blood of Christ,
and the bright afternoon sun
burst through the curtains
in a blinding moment of
just being alive.
There is no other time than this.

Bathing in the sea
by the rocks
after a Dead show,
I was seeing into the nature of things—
the beach was made sacred by it,
so too the waves and my body
dissolving into each other
as the sky and time became
a miraculous atomic soup.

This is it.

The blood and amniotic fluid
on my wife's leg
and the hospital bed
were blessed by it
and the awestruck faces
of strangers wondering
at my son's first breath and cry

along with the salt of the tears
on our faces.

This is it.

Seeing the last troubled breath
of the dying,
bleeding the dense texture of joy,
nursing deep silence,
finding the space
where words come to being
and there is nothing but
the thing itself,
the precious gap in time between
longing and action.
In all of our heedlessness
and earnest searching,
sometimes we get lucky
and stumble into it,
landing squarely inside
the beating heart of the instant
and it is
full, radiant—
right now,
outside your window,
inside
your
skull.

Sunday Morning in Golden Hill

Sitting with my coffee
in the back room with
a view of the bottlebrush tree,
I hear sirens racing
towards somebody else's pain
and the sound of an airplane
cruising in to land at the airport,
leaving the air swirling
in its wake.

Then, for a moment,
silence,
before the voices of a gospel choir
rise from the church
down the street
and join the birds in the tree
in the backyard
along with the woman
humming
as she takes laundry down
the stairs of the apartment complex
across the alley—
all of them singing,
beautifully together,
on this fine
Sunday morning.

In the Lees of Things

It comes to me slowly,
never in an elegant place,
but by the motel pool,
wet and disheveled,
staring at the sun on the water,
or half asleep
in the side yard
awkwardly splayed on
a plastic lawn chair.

Time slows down
and each instant
gains a deep resonance—
a ripple in stillness,
a red brick
layered with fine dust
and fall leaves,
the feeling of cool sweat
on skin,
the silence at the heart
of all noise.

The joy it brings
is
so thick
it almost has a taste,
but I can never
hold onto it,
not even for a
second.

Chasing the Heart of the Instant

Waking at 5:00 AM to sit and breathe
in the pale dawn,
sipping coffee
like it was
redemption itself.
First the rhythm of taking in air
and exhaling,
then the feel of the body,
the pain in my back and legs
and a thousand other little things
I endure to get to the
center of my struggle,
to tear myself apart,
touch the core of my grief,
fear, and shame.
There they are—
the anger and helplessness.
How fragile the edifice that is
my dream of self.
I sit tight and focus
on the suffering of those
I hold dear as well
as those I hate.
I sit and breathe and caress the source
of my longing and
see that it is depthless
and that I am
hopelessly driven
by the devil of
white hot desire.
The baby cries next door,
a siren blares,
and I hear a loud conversation
about where to get breakfast.

I lose focus and drift toward
the same petty garbage
in my head,
despair at my fucking hopelessness
but bring myself back
to my in-breath,
get into a rhythm,
achieve a few seconds
of not spinning away.
I finish and open my eyes
to the bare white wall,
slowly, painfully
straighten my legs and rise,
wincing from the stiffness.

This is not nirvana.

But later that day, I hear a bird's sweet song,
notice how light hits
a tree in the late afternoon
and makes it luminous.
This stops me, the splendor.
I soak in the fragile, transient feeling of that voluptuous few seconds—
the sound and color
and untranslatable presentness.

If I could, I would bleed the essence
of that moment
forever.
But it's always on to the next one
and the one after that
and I chase them all
hoping to stumble
into something
that reminds me
I'm alive
if only for one
gorgeous
instant.

The Caves at Lava Beds National Monument

From the sweltering July heat
I descended into the cave,
past the petroglyphs
marking the mouth of the entrance,
into the first chamber
similarly adorned with
ancient geometric shapes,
mysterious symbols,
and evocative patterns
whose origins no Anglo ethnographer bothered
to inquire after.
Then, the Modoc were slaughtered,
and the survivors relocated
in the 19th century
of American Progress.
Perhaps, the signs note,
these images were
part of a creation story
or marked a religious observance.

I made my way further
into the depths of the cavern
and the air was cooler
as I squeezed through
narrow crevices in the rocks
and entered sheer darkness
lit only by my feeble headlamp.
It was icy cold now and
I shivered while carefully
sliding down
a smooth wall of stone
to the bottom.

There, a small body
of still water
lay frozen.
I ran my hand across
the mirror-like ice
with reverence.
Perching at the edge of the pool,
I turned off my headlight
to take in the impenetrable,
black silence.

Before the conquest,
the Modoc came here
and had visions
in this underground
dream space.
Perhaps they spoke to the dead
or took some measure
of the sacred
they believed lived
all around them.

Now, as I sat
in the cold bowels
of the earth,
I felt my heart beating,
in the void
and was seized by a mixture
of terror and awe
amidst the frigid rock
and the heart
of everything
that is.

Last Summer in the Sierras

It was a dazzling, hot summer morning
as we set off
down the path to the trailhead
and the hike
into the mountains
through the welcome shade
of dense pines.
We took one step after another
up the increasingly steep incline.
My head swam and sweat
rolled down my forehead
into my eyes.
I could taste the salt in my mouth
and forged on,
trying to keep pace with my son
bounding forward
with his long legs
and lanky frame.

This was the boy
I used to have to carry
on my shoulders
after less than a mile.

When the going got arduous,
now I watched him
from behind as
he strode on
effortlessly
across a huge bridge
of boulders,
stopping only at the summit
to gaze at a higher peak
that rose out of the ravine

below us.
Around a bend in the trail
we hit the top of a waterfall
and felt the spray refresh us
as it bounced up off
the jagged rocks below.

We stopped in a nook
by the rushing river,
dunked our heads
in a pool of cold water,
and lay back on
a bed of stone
to watch the world
glitter and dance
in the radiant light
of midday,
my son's wild wet hair
glistening in the sunshine.

This was our last summer together
before he left home
to start his new life,
leaving me to wander
the ruins of myself,
trying to let go
of my attachment
and crushing grief.

The way back was brutally hot, dusty,
and longer than I had remembered.
My whole body ached to the bone.

That night at camp,
we ate beans from a tin can
and sat together,
chatting and staring up
at the endless, star-filled sky
that always makes you feel

small and vast
at the same time.

"How much pain and sweetness
can fit into one man's life?"
I thought before limping
to my tent and
sleeping
like the dead.

Naked

We wake from restless sleep
in the pitch dark,
sweating, hearts racing,
our two heads spinning
in their own separate hells,
helplessly charting the waters
of uncertainty and fear
in the long shadow
of my possible end.
I can hear you quietly weeping,
and I search for your hand,
and find it, warm and tender,
a naked thing lost in the black night.
We embrace
without words,
and lie together, breathing deeply,
desperately hoping for the release of slumber.
Slowly, in unison, we drift off,
as if dying, blissfully,
in the arms of a love
beyond desire.

Into the Bardo

After Pema Chödrön

During the dawning hours,
I struggled to sleep,
failing to catch even
a stray minute of peace.
Throughout it all
my nurse, Jeff, said to me,
in his calm, steady voice,
"Go with the river,
you can't fight the river,
go with the river."
He repeated it, over and over,
like a mantra,
and his words stayed with me
throughout the night,
into the early morning
and onward to this day.

Before they came to take me to surgery,
I said to my son, "If I don't make it, remember to
look at your hand and I'll be there, always."
My wife wiped away my tears, kissed me,
and, as they wheeled me down the hallway,
I recalled what I told my son the day before,
as I cradled his head in my hands,
"Be not afraid, have courage, and be steadfast."

But in my gut, I was sure I would die.

Death was smiling at me in the darkness,
waiting patiently by my side,
whispering to me that
it was time to pass over,

quietly and quickly,
to his lonely kingdom.

"It will be a delicate and difficult procedure,"
I heard a surgeon say in the operating room,
thinking that I had already gone under.

So, I lay there, on the razor's edge.
Now, I knew I had
no time, no time, no time
to waste—

Not. One. Moment. More.

My body had been screaming this for months,
and now the doctors knew it too
as they spoke in a semi-whisper,
"Let's start the procedure."
As the anesthesia took hold,
I occupied a space between life and death,
tiptoeing along the border,
trying to impose a semblance of order
on my inner chaos.
I held tightly to the discipline of
just breathing in and out,
in and out,
deeply and slowly,
and letting whatever came to be
sit there as it was.

Suddenly, I reached a strange state
of grace
and went blank.

My last thought,
before the six-hour caesura,
was of teaching Hemingway's
"A Clean Well-Lighted Place"
in a classroom with a view
of a distant tree

shedding a few
reluctant autumn leaves
in the soft breeze.

And then deep nothingness, suspended from time.

Still lying on my back,
I came to consciousness,
furtively, eyes closed,
silently repeating to myself
a line from Pema Chödrön,
"How we live is how we die,"
which I seamlessly replaced
with a memory of my nurse
slowly guiding me forward,
"Don't fight the river, go with it.
You can't fight the river,
let it flow through you."

Amen.

Stars

Perhaps you won't believe me,
but there were stars behind my eyes
as I sat in meditation
in the darkness of our back room,
listening to the rain pouring down,
baptizing the broken world
and my mind after
weeks of being battered by pain,
sleeplessness, exhaustion, delirium,
seizures, psychotic breaks, and
the haunting memory of the
sheer panic on the faces of my beloveds,
my wife and son, summoning the courage
to weather the storm—
like the beleaguered crew of a
galleon of old,
battening down the hatches,
and securing the deck
as they held on for dear life.

But now, I kept my eyes closed
and my body melted
as the top of my head opened
revealing the vastness of the universe beyond
the stars.
Then I felt, intuited more than saw,
the interconnectedness of all things,
like a loving embrace
that transcended the physical,
but leveled me with awe
and left me stunned by the
thereness of it,
naked, egoless,
not knowing names or

any word that could capture
the essence of it.

As I came back to myself,
eyes still shut,
the stars took on a
a deep glow.
And I remember that it was my wife's face
I was tenderly stroking,
trembling with adoration.
The sound of the rain falling,
drop after drop
on the roof of
our shabby Craftsman house,
splashing the fragile windowpanes,
as the warm breeze
from the tropical storm came in,
all of it blending into a joyous song
that fused with my breath
and became a
deep, resonant humming,
that seeped into the core
of that thing I call me
but is really everything
that is.
And it all started
glowing, glowing, glowing.
Then, when I opened my eyes,
the luminosity persisted,
framing the edges of the windows
and sitting like a crown atop the extended
branches of the bottlebrush tree
swaying outside in the wind.

My wife's face and body were resplendent
as were the richly grained panels of hardwood
in the floor as
I walked down the hallway.
And it continued when I lay down in bed,
the whole world aglow,

dancing with radiance.
As I switched off the light,
the stars were back behind my eyes,
and they lingered there until
I slipped away into emptiness,
smiling.

What Was It Like?

So what was it like,
almost dying?

It was like falling out
of the world,
away from the vast horizons
and the loving embrace
of crowds of beautiful strangers—
the books of their lives
written on their faces—
losing sight of the
gorgeous monsters of cities,
and the paths
that take you away from them
to the shade of old trees
and the greenness of grass
growing amidst
weathered stones.

It was like tumbling away
from myself
into small spaces in rooms—
a spot on a bed,
hours of the false comfort of sheets
and warm covers—
then slowly,
bit by bit,
losing strength, sleep,
good humor,
hunger,
and worst of all,
desire.

It was watching myself recede,
losing grasp of my mind,
my hold over sentences,
the intimate touch of words,
and concentration—
becoming nothing but
breath and sight
and bottomless grief
like falling down a hole
with no way out
as the voices of
my beloveds
grew faint
in the far distance.

It was the blank stillness of night
with only the sound of
my heart pounding fiercely.

It's arriving at a place where
you realize that you control
nothing,
not your body, your emotions, your mind.
Helpless and trembling,
you shiver at the emptiness
at your core,
the realization
that you have no core
but are instead
a dry fallen leaf
floating on the surface of
a restless river,
gliding until you
sink
and are just the river
or really a speck of
the atomic soup
of water
or what we think

is water
rather than merely a part
of the flow of things
beyond time.

Underneath the fear
there is surrender and release.
Not so much ecstasy or joy
but abandon and drift.

You are
simply
not
there.

And how did it feel
to live again?

It was amazement at
the sweetness of apple juice
and the delicious bite of bitter coffee
blended with the sharpness of
a thousand needle pricks
in my arm,
and the feel
of my stapled torso.
It was loving the texture
of all that we feel,
even the mysterious
contours of pain.

It was the touch
of my lover's hand,
the smell of my son's hair
as he bent over me,
the taste of the thick
salt of tears.

It was struggling to sit up,
so weak after losing

sixty pounds in six days,
being helped to eat slowly
and then, most important of all,
to walk,
step after step
on the cold tile floor
of the hospital,
the creaky hardwood
in my house,
and the broken pavement
of the sidewalk outside—
seeing the Mexican poppies
blooming in the yard,
hearing the whiz
and twitter of hummingbirds,
feeling the tender blades of grass
underneath my bare feet.

And, as it went on,
the world came back,
one footstep
at a time—
the families at the taco shop,
neighbors walking dogs,
the huge, unruly ficus
in the park
where the lawn is full of rabbits at dawn,
hawks soaring across the canyon,
and the ruins of
the beautiful fountain
by the pathway
that winds down the hillside
past a sea of orange flowers.

It was holding
my wife's hand in mine
as my gait
became steady,
hearing the dirt crunch
under the soles of my shoes,

knowing that everything we need
is always
right here
in front of us.

This One Small Life

If one day
the blood I spit in the sink
turns out to mean that
I'm dying,
what will this
one small life,
this stream of continuous
moments
that are me
amount to?

As much as we try
to trap ourselves
into a snapshot
in time,
we cannot be measured
or defined by
grief, joy, anger, boredom,
or any of the
myriad moods
that flow through us.

I am not my dying
or becoming,
not agony, ecstasy,
dignity, despair, desire,
pride, envy or humility.
Nor am I triumphant, transcendent,
or absurd—
just all these things
running together
in the flux.

I am made of memories
of running through
the orange groves,
open fields,
rocky hillsides,
green forests,
and sandy beaches
of my childhood.

I am the ballfields,
basketball courts,
grid irons,
grass, dirt, sweat,
and bloody fights
of early contests—
the sound of the baseball
in the glove
and off the bat,
the feel of hitting
and being hit,
the easy grace
and quick movement
of my youthful body,
the sound of sneakers squeaking
on the court,
the basketball leaving my hands
as I leap through
the air.

I am the endless
shelves of books
I've read,
the ocean of words,
phrases, sentences,
and passages pored
over, again and again—
Whitman, Lispector, Neruda,
Kerouac, Thich Nhat Hanh,
Knausgaard, Miller, Kafka,

Duras, Baldwin, Oliver,
and on and on.

All the flashes of insight,
meditative moments,
thoughts that cut
deep and hard,
the beauty that cracked
the shell of myself
and left me exposed
to the black of night
and the glory of
the new day,
the unspeakable brilliance
of stars
and the burning heat
of the sun.

The music too is me—
the sounds that crept
into the forgotten corners
of my being
and grew deep roots there
like the silence between
trumpet notes of Miles Davis,
the lilting rise
of Jerry Garcia's guitar,
slow blues,
tender plaintive voices,
the rush of jubilant, ecstatic noise,
jams, dub, punk, and spare acoustic strumming,
the geometric precision of Bach,
and the forgotten
wonders of melody.

And the art is me—
seeing things just like Robert Frank
on a lonely American highway,
Van Gogh in the garden,

Vermeer peering into the pantry
through a side window.

The funky old houses are me—
Craftsman, Victorian, Spanish style
along with the Modernist landmarks
and the spare lines
that frame the studio
down the street.
I've walked by them all
and every wandering step is made
of longing, curiosity,
and the melancholy light
of a late fall afternoon
in the park.

The millions of footsteps
exploring the insides of buildings,
classrooms, union halls, picket lines,
hotels, and ballparks in cities,
and the open spaces outside them,
under the cover of redwoods by the sea,
across the desert, up alpine trails,
or by farms and patches of wildflowers.

I've seen there the faces of animals,
the gladness and glory
of their movements—
the sweet eyes of deer,
the lumbering carriage of bears,
and the delicate poetry of birdsong.
I love them all and their brethren
are part of me.
I see myself in
the woodland critters and sea creatures—
the grand elk, big horn sheep,
jack rabbits, chipmunks,
turtles, dolphins,
grey whales, starfish, urchins
and snails

along with a host of animals
lost to the world.
I mourn the vanished,
love and remember them
with bittersweet fondness.

What will the world be
without you?

I too am the faces I've kissed,
the breasts suckled,
thighs stroked,
and bodies that have engulfed me.
Is there a more holy place
than where we touch each other
naked and alone together
as our skin tingles,
and flesh engorges and merges
with the other?
I am those intimate caresses
as well as bear hugs,
pats on the back,
hands on shoulders, and
the wonderfully
terrifying moments
when our eyes
lock into each other
and share everything
and more
without words.

I am you, sisters and brothers,
And you are me—
groping from minute to minute,
second by second—
newborn, child, adolescent,
young adult, middle-aged,
old and dying.
I am mother, father, child,
parent, grandparent,

and all those who came before
and will come after
are me,
right now—
staring at the blood in the sink
and knowing it is
our time
but not wanting it to be—
yearning for just one more
perfect fall morning
when there is dawn in me,
one more gentle twilight sky
as I sit on the porch
and lose myself
in the deep glowing red
between the branches
of the grand old pine tree
as cars roll by honking,
ambulances screaming,
and the wings of birds
fluttering above me
like a miracle
as profound as any other
day we have
for as long as we
are still breathing
and deeply adoring the air
that bathes this precious, beautiful,
horrifying, grace-filled world we share.

My blood, your blood,
everyone's blood
flows together
and apart
in unison,
feeding the life
we witness
and hold tenderly
for how long
we don't know.

I just know that
this very instant
has always been
and will always be
so full and
glowing with love
that it blinds us
to see it.

This Much I Know About Desire

The Wild Years

What were you looking for
when I followed your yearning,
crossing the border,
drifting into
the Zona Norte
in the lost hours
of early morning
after the American bars closed?

Were you looking for a way
out of time
as we wandered
through teeming streets
past taco stands
and storefront churches,
in and out of bars
until I didn't
know my name?

Were you looking for sorrow
as we drank in cantinas
built with stone sadness
and danced with shy women
who no one remembered?

Were you looking for evil
as you talked with hustlers,
took turns down dark alleys,
lost me
and wound up fallen and bloody
in a sordid apartment
doing crystal with prostitutes
while a man kneeled
to huff paintas if in prayer?

Were you looking for peace
when by chance I found you
in a dungeon-like bar
where we smoked Delicados
before ascending to dawn—
the street bathed in gentle pink
as two tired women
in bright blue
and red dresses
stood quietly,
yawning, waiting for food
while Mayan children
dreamt on the sidewalk
and smoke rose from the grill
like a soul toward heaven
and we stopped for a moment
stunned
by a beautiful
stillness?

On the Way to Jai Alai Palace, Tijuana, Mexico

The turnstiles
clang as I
walk across the
border into Tijuana,
head through the
throng of cab drivers
asking if I want
"pharmacy," "disco,"
or "donkey show."
I walk past
the women
selling ceramic Pooh bears,
wool blankets,
Guatemalan purses,
and switch blades.
The smell of
carne asada
from the taquerias
mixes with
cigarette smoke drifting
over from
the outdoor sportsbook
where a crowd of
men stand staring at
TVs with results
from Santa Anita,
holding Styrofoam cups
of coffee,
Tecates, and
rolled-up newspapers.

I walk across the
bridge over
the river
where the poor
live in boxes
and perish
with winter rains.

On the other side,
as I go down
the steps,
small children are
begging for change,
tugging on the leg
of my pants.
I give my last
quarter to
a little girl
with big round eyes
and the band follows me
for another half block.
Back on the street
I listen
to the sound of buses
and cars and the shopkeepers
hawking t-shirts, leather goods,
bird cages, and
laundry baskets.
There are signs for
cut-rate Prozac
and Cuban cigars,
and I'm struck by
the sight of
a church steeple
in the distance,
set off
against the deep
red sky.
At the corner,

I look down the street
into the Zona Norte,
turn the other way and
start toward
the Jai Alai Palace.

On Avenida Revolución,
there are
tourists and vendors
and pictures
with the zebra-striped
donkey.
It's early and
the discos are
loud and empty.
I pass by
the barkers for
a stripshow
and look
up at the
MOTEL
sign in the
new night sky,
lit up and flashing
blue, red, yellow,
white and green.
I stop at a
folk art stand,
regard a series
of skeletons
carved for
el Dia de los Muertos:
Death performing surgery,
Death shooting baskets,
Death smoking at the typewriter.
Then I hear a voice
on a scratchy loudspeaker
shouting out,
"Feliz Navidad! Feliz Navidad!"
And I turn around

to see the parade
coming down the street—
a few small boys dressed
as Christmas trees
and dozens of little angels,
all in white dresses,
filling the night
with the light
of their laughter.
And for a moment,
everything stops.
Shopkeepers step
out of their storefronts
and the buzz of pedestrians
pauses and smiles.

Once the procession
passes I enter
the sportsbook
at the Jai Alai Palace—
I note the Art Deco style,
the familiar haze
of smoke and
the smell of stale beer.
At the book
I put $40
on the Lakers and over,
lose badly,
and think
of the
angels.

Holiday

I wake up in my
motel room
on Thanksgiving morning
and hear
the maid in the room next door
cleaning the tub,
taking out garbage.
At breakfast,
the cook, the waiter
and the owner
of the empty diner
serve me,
their only customer,
and make small talk
about the holidays
while the owner obsessively
polishes the counter
and puts up
the day's special:
"Turkey with gravy,
stuffing, rolls."
I think about the cheerful,
polite American loneliness
and the work
the work
the work
of stolen
lives.

Bombay Beach, CA

At midday
it was 105 and
the wind was blowing the
stench off
the Salton Sea.
There was an old pick-up
outside the general store
with a sticker about Jesus
on the tailgate.
As I drove through
the tiny grid of streets,
I passed two lonely
little churches
that could have been
auto parts stores.
Most of the trailer homes
were empty
but a few had the AC on,
rattling away,
laboring hard against
the inferno outside
as the people stayed cool
and built mystery
behind blinds.
Toward the shore,
the road turned to gravel
and I stopped to look
at the lifeless shell of
a bar
with the open sign
still hanging from the window.
By the abandoned marina,
there were houses and trailers
half-submerged in the rancid water,

victims of a past flood
after winter rains.
I got out of
the car and walked down
a decaying pier,
the flies hovering
in a cloud
around my head,
the water
full of dead corvina
and other fish
perishing slowly,
their gills
struggling to move
a few last times.
And from above,
a solitary pelican was swooping down,
feasting on the easy prey.

I looked out, across the sea.
It was strangely beautiful—
the eerie glow of the sun and heat
on the water
framed by distant mountains
and the vast, empty desert.
Turning back to the car,
I saw two figures
fishing in the distance.
An old man,
uncannily reminiscent of
John Lee Hooker
in his final years,
and a tiny boy,
who must have been his grandson,
sitting in lawn chairs,
holding their lines
and grabbing
Cokes from
a cooler

as if no one had told them
about the end of the world.

I got back in the car
and drove to the highway,
windows up,
AC on.
The radio said that birds
were dying
of an unknown disease.

A Mile Before Mecca

Driving into the impending twilight
about a mile before Mecca
I came upon the charred ruins of
the Sundowner Motel,
a Texas Barbeque sign still hanging
in the lone surviving window
of the dead lounge.
I pulled off the highway,
parked my car,
and strolled through the wreckage—
abandoned wheels
from a roll-away bed,
a blackened freezer full of ash,
old beer cans,
box springs, and the hollowed-out shell
of an air conditioner.

Under a rock I saw
an unspoiled page from a porno magazine—
two buxom blonds embroiled in a banal,
calculated embrace against
a lurid purple backdrop.
A few feet away
were the want ads
from the *Los Angeles Times*
with a call for
"winners with attitude"
to do telemarketing.
Then the dusty, drained pool
in the midst of a patio with
"No lifeguard on duty."

I kicked a broken porcelain fixture
and gazed at the rusty iron stairs

leading up to nowhere.
The sun was setting,
low and crimson,
and the desert was still,
empty at the core.

Processional

It was Easter Sunday
on Highway 111
by the decaying shore
of the Salton Sea
and the head-on collision
left the driver of the pick-up
and the whole family in the van
dead.

Strange to see the blood
on the windshields
and the horrible collage
of metal and flesh
so intimately
as the cop directed
the long line of traffic
onward, slowly,
with each car
creeping up solemnly
for a furtive glimpse
at the carnage
before driving on
to someplace else.

What I noticed was
a little girl's hand
pushed up against
the passenger side window,
her tiny fingers
still clutching
a single red rose.

Remembrance of Things Past

I thought he was dead
but I saw him
at the corner of 11th and Broadway
by the closed-down pool hall
over the Limerick Room.
He walked out of the bar
and passed my car
as I waited on a red light—
his gaunt Creole face
under a weathered ballcap,
sweat beading
on his forehead before
streaming down
high cheekbones
in July heat.
He was thinner now,
wiry, but moving
with a steady grace,
light-footed,
almost ghostly.

I watched him walk
down the street
toward Market
and remembered
seven years ago
as if it was still happening—
the way he put down his beer
before heading for the door,
smiled vaguely
with longing in his eyes
and told me
"every day feels
like the end of the world."

Ritual

I worked the door there
for a year
and at least once a week
he'd get drunk
and tell me
I looked like his son—
the one who came back from 'Nam
scored a job on the force,
got married
and had three kids
before one day,
without reason,
he came home from work
to a dark empty house
and ate the barrel
of his gun
in the lonely shadows
of evening.
Every time he told me
I'd look at him—
his bleary brown eyes
streaming with tears
that he'd wipe
with thick fingers
stained black with grease
and marred
by small cuts
that never seemed
to heal.

Blues

After too much coffee
at a place
downtown
I walk home.
I am long-haired,
unshaven,
torn shirt,
dirty jeans.
Still, they can smell
the money on me.
I give away 15, 25, 40
cents on G,
turn the corner at 5th near
the porno theaters
and walk by a block of
men on the street,
give away all of
the rest of my change.
At 5th and F
I say, "Sorry, busted man."
"How 'bout a cig?"
"Don't smoke,"
"Take it up. . .
you don't wanna live through
this shit."
I stare into dead brown eyes,
a crowd of dead brown eyes.

He steps up,
into my face,
"Why you wanna live through
this shit man?"
He means it.
"I'm hangin' in,"

I say feeling
stupid and white
and crossing the street.

Now I'm wired, tense, I
notice the way
blank-eyed blue suits
walk out of bars, offices,
restaurants, with
caged eyes, hands over pockets,
rushed and purposeful feet.
(And I know
this is nothing new) but
I notice (as if for
the first time) a ragged
old woman pushing
a shopping cart,
the smell of piss on the sidewalk,
the way some people
at the bus stop
wait stoic and tired, the
way others are timid, scared,
the way others still,
sneer at me.
Then I see the way women
are afraid at night,
glancing backwards, clutching
their purses.

And there is so much of everything,
so many
cars and banks and businesses,
so many big signs
and pretty lights,
and I think, "You don't
wanna live through this shit man."
And I've got a certain kind of
American sadness,
that cuts to
the bone.

Death at the Astor Hotel

They turn
only for a split-second,
most not at all.
Once the siren stops wailing
and the flashing red lights
are clicked off,
the hurried waitress
in a bright yellow dress
glances out
the greasy window of
the place across the street.
The fat cop
at the parking meter
looks up from
a license plate
or some guy
waiting at a stoplight
in a '68 Dodge
cracks the side vent
and taps a cigarette
in the direction of
the Astor Hotel
as they come down
the steps to pop the
sheet-covered stretcher
in back,
but only for a split second,
leaving the bed unmade,
the paper on the floor,
a water glass
still sitting
on the
nightstand.

At the Waterfront, 1990

Walking down Grape Street
toward the harbor
the sun is blinding,
brilliant gold on the water,
and I'm taken
with the street,
smiling at children
playing on the tiny lawns
of little green houses
by the freeway,
listening to the stereo
of a battered Ford pick-up
blasting corridos
que dicen,
"No tengo dinero."
The men
on the porch
have deep lines
around their eyes
and joy in their hearts
on Sunday,
and the women
are laughing and dancing
and singing along.
At the Waterfront
I order machaca and beer
and stare at fading pictures
of boxers and fishermen,
the boats at the docks
when they used to catch tuna.
The Depression, the war,
the sun-weathered faces
and calloused hands
are long gone.

Now tourists walk
the sidewalks
by the bay
with bored spouses,
trying to forget
their lives
and manage restless,
well-dressed children.
The machaca is good—
hot and filling.
I look out the window
at a rundown house
across the street
as the jukebox
begins to play
bad love songs
that mix with the sound
of the waitress
picking up plates
and empty glasses
from the tables.
She sets them down
on the counter
and stops to pull back
her raven hair,
and rubs the back of her neck—
beautiful
without knowing it.

December 24th, 1997

At the last minute,
I walk downtown
past a man
sweeping broken ornaments
off the sidewalk
outside
the homeless shelter,
making a pile of
shards of green glass.
I look at
my watch,
see it's 4:50,
walk faster,
and notice
the cook staring out
the window of
the Chicken Shack,
people milling into
old churches.
I pass
tailored suits
with cocktails
at the Horton Grand Hotel,
and a teenage girl
with dyed-green hair,
a nose ring, and a
tight pink shirt
that says:
"Jesus is coming,
look busy."
Twilight is falling
and I can see
the blood red sky
fading to black

in the mirrored glass
of a nameless high-rise.
There are multi-colored
Christmas trees
on the tops of banks
and blinking white lights
around a little window
in a rooming house.
At 4th and Broadway
in the park by
the mall,
a man is asking
fleeing shoppers
for change
in a voice so faint
that none of them hear him
as they rush
toward cars and
freeways and
pastel houses
that all look the same.
It's then that I glance down
at the paper rack
and see the headline
in the *Union*:
"Gunmen slaughter
Mexican peasants—
dozens of Indians
killed in
Chiapas."
When I reach my destination,
they shut the door
in my face
at 5:00 PM sharp.
Still no room
in the Inn.

Costs

What are the costs?
Ask the man with a
band-aid over the hole in
his face where his nose was
as he stands by the stairs
of the post office downtown,
adjusting his wrinkled
ballcap,
clutching a rolled newspaper,
trying not to meet the eyes
of passersby.
Ask the sullen old
woman gazing into
her empty PO box,
shutting it slowly,
carefully, before turning away
to a room full of strangers,
the street outside,
and another day
marked by pointless rituals.
How long do we pay?
Ask the cowboy
in a dirty rhinestone shirt
and a ten-gallon hat
sitting on the garbage can
in front of the library,
watching cars pass,
not asking for change
as people walk by
with suspicious eyes
and arms full of books.
Ask the woman with
the bloodied nose,
cursing her lover as

he strides down the street
and nobody stops him
as the crimson
drops
hit the sidewalk.
Why do we hope?
Ask the waitress
leaving work, glancing up
at Christmas lights
on the grand old building
where she can't afford dinner.
Ask the wandering homeless,
the insane,
the man stopping traffic
as he walks against a red,
a tattered book
in his hand,
screaming—
I only heard this—
"Unless the dream comes!"

Asbestos

At lunchtime
I look out the huge
warehouse doors
and watch the teenage girls
at the bus stop.
I'm sick of endless rows of boxes
and the dull threatening smell.
I'm sick of that thick crust
of dust and grease
which mixes with the sweat of my body
and never seems to come off.
Coring brake shoes
at a warehouse in Van Nuys,
I read the health warning:
Asbestos.
I stick my head deep down
into the rusty barrel—
I reach for a shoe,
smell the dust,
feel it on my skin,
and spit the taste from
my mouth.
Pulling it out,
I see it rise.
Holding my breath,
I work faster.

The Pantry

It's like 1935 here
and nothing's
as good as
a big fat T-bone
served up
by Dizzy
or Big Leo
with a smart-ass joke
and black coffee.
Their gilded sign
proudly tells you—
"Never closed since 1924.
We've killed enough chickens
to feed all of Los Angeles."
Something more
than grease beat
the Great Depression.
You still see it
in the way they walk
briskly between chairs
to pour coffee.
It gets passed on.
Now
there are young men
pouring coffee
and down 6th Avenue
it's cold—
men are huddled over
barrel fires.
Someone warms his hands,
retreats
to curl fetus-like
in a doorway.
It gets passed on.

Work

Having run out
of lies,
my father fights
the cool gray morning.
After Seagram's and OJ,
he loads the truck
with tools,
guns the engine,
and turns on radio news.
Today we will work
in old houses—
patch holes in walls,
mend fences,
re-tile floors.
When the owners come,
he'll talk shit,
jack the price.

Father, if I could,
I'd take the sneer off
the face of the world,
bring back the lush green
fields of your childhood,
make the work simple and good.

Now there is only driving.
Every day harder,
a little less will.
We do not speak.
His hands covered
with tiny scars,
he steers the truck,
stares blankly
at the road.

Lifeblood

Fixing his car
on the street
in the dark
on a Monday night
before work,
he feels cold metal
blindly,
moves a dim flashlight
with his other hand
until he comes upon
the right bolt.
Old and rusted,
it snaps
despite
WD-40
and patience.
He stands up
too quickly,
hits his head
on the hood,
and curses under his breath.
As he rubs his scalp
he finds blood
and looks at it—
crimson red
on his fingertips.
The parts store is closed,
the bills are months late,
and the job
never ends.

Twenty-Six Doors

I get off for my transfer
at the downtown terminal,
steal a smile from a
pretty young woman
and her boyfriend glares
so I just keep walking
by the rows of black chairs
with little TVs on them
where people are staring at
football, car commercials,
Gilligan's Island.
I've got 40 minutes to watch
a pimp
sweet talk some innocent child
(coming or going, I'm not sure)
and look at the line of payphones—
the elderly white ladies checking in,
waiting with fat suitcases,
the nervous guy who
doesn't want me to listen
and puts his hand
over the side of his mouth.
I go get a burger
at SNACK BAR
lit with '50s neon,
play Pac Man in
FUNLAND ARCADE,
and get a picture
in the photo booth.
Later a sailor wants
change for a one.
I watch him
buy a Pepsi,
a Mounds bar and

share it with a woman
who looks Vietnamese—
her eyes smiling above
the can as she drinks.
There are people standing,
waiting at twenty-six doors.
Las Vegas, Bakersfield, San Fernando
all have their portion
of tired feet and
hands in back pockets.
The TV-posted times
are always wrong,
but they're used to it,
standing, waiting
at twenty-six doors.
I think of the lives,
of berry fields,
assembly lines,
dirty kitchens,
and cash registers.
I think about the
dull creeping misery
and joy rare
as fine wine,
and it's timeless
somehow,
always with us,
like a cruel museum.

L.A.

Santa Ana winds
blow in at midnight,
banishing
rain clouds
and smog.
They kiss my face,
run fingers
through my hair,
and show me stars I've never seen
through the bare branches
of trees.

Volunteers

People will farm in the morning,
make music in the afternoon, and
fuck wherever and whenever they want to.
—Jerry Rubin, *Do It!*

They still come here—
I saw a little card
posted on the bulletin board
at the Anarchist Collective Bookstore
in Haight Ashbury.
It said:
"AIDS victim,
Needs Understanding—
Quiet place to die.
Can pay."
Outside it was twilight.
The world felt cold and unreal
and I wondered how we live.

Toledo, Ohio, USA

You leave the empty depot
looking for food
and walk by boarded-up
storefronts,
abandoned factories,
crumbling red brick warehouses,
and churches where
rocks broke the
eyes of God.
And then you find it,
a place where they
play tired blues
and serve greasy burgers
with beer
that pours flat
from the tap.
The waiter's friendly,
and people talk through
the music,
laughing too loud
in thick flannel shirts
and boots
still dripping from snow.
The old man who plays saxophone
falls asleep between solos,
his cigarette still burning,
hanging from his lips
by a thread.
Outside,
under the leaden sky,
a bitter wind whips up
off the Maumee River,
slapping your face,
killing the warmth

from the beer.
They used to make scales here,
blow glass,
assemble spark plugs,
but nobody walks
these streets
anymore.

House of Blues, Chicago, Illinois

For Luther Allison and James Baldwin

Luther Allison
dished out
a searing blues
for well-dressed
white couples
on dates
while stoic Black women
took coats in
the lobby.
He talked and played
for an hour longer
than the crowd
could dance and
drink.
"Y'all know
about pain?"
he asked them,
resting his hand
lightly
on the neck
of his guitar,
sweat dripping
down his face.
"Pain is
what it's
all about
people."
His eyes were
elsewhere,
looking at
and through
the faces
by the stage.

"I'm talkin' 'bout
deep down
soul pain,
real *hurt*."
The crowd cheered,
but he didn't smile
as he dug down
a little deeper
and made the
guitar wail and moan,
his face like
the very heart
of yearning.

Outside it was cold.
I hailed a cab.
The driver said,
"Fucking tourists,"
as he passed
a car with
out-of-state plates.
We drove through
the Gold Coast,
across the ornate bridge
over the Chicago River,
past the grand
historic buildings
and mirrored glass,
Harold's Chicken Shack,
the Rescue Mission.

On the way,
I thought about
the storm inside,
the two cities
and the death
of hope.

Back at the hotel
I stared

out the window
at the lights
of the city,
the tiny figures,
four stories below
on the 3 AM street.
When I closed my eyes
I could still hear
the guitar
weeping,
falling down
like pouring rain.
Luther was dead by August
and the world
keeps making
pain.

Corktown, Detroit

There's an old church
in the parking lot
where the neighborhood once was
and the fading paint
on the backs
of brick buildings
reminds you
of immigrants
who moved to the suburbs
leaving
gas stations and
liquor stores
with bulletproof glass,
empty storefronts,
check cashing signs,
and burned-out blocks
from Devil's night.

After the game,
I take a walk
down the street to
the last few blocks
of Corktown
where the retired
and the hopeful
tend to quaint
little gardens
and postage-stamp lawns
as the sky darkens
and a thunderstorm
gathers above.
I smile at an elderly woman
clipping red roses
in front of

the Victorian house
on the corner,
stop
and stare at
a barren warehouse
across the way.
"They win?"
asks the woman
who's noticed my cap.
"No," I say
and head back
to my car
still sitting in
a lot behind
a deserted bar
and the ghost of
a restaurant
that used to serve
ribs and homestyle
chicken.
By now the lot
is vacant.
Puddles are forming
in muddy potholes
and behind the car,
in the midst of
the lost space
between boarded-up buildings,
I notice a light
in the window
of a solitary house
on the desolate street
that once was
a block teeming with crowds.

The thunder claps hard,
like the hands
of God,
but the man outside
is still mowing

his lawn
slowly, carefully,
ignoring
the lightening
exploding in the
late summer sky.
It's raining hard now
but I stay
outside the car,
looking at the man,
breathing in
the smell of the
dense wet air,
feeling
the warm rain
on my face.

Kalispell, Montana

I woke
before dawn,
heard a noise
and pulled back
the shade in my hotel room
to see a man in overalls
loading lumber
and tools
into the bed
of an old pick-up
behind the hardware store
next door.
It was late August
but still cold enough
to see
his breath
as he labored to lift
one 2x4 after another
into the truck.
When he was done,
he stopped, sighed,
and took a tin
of tobacco
out of his back pocket,
put a pinch
in his mouth,
rubbed his thick beard,
spit,
and mumbled something
to himself
I couldn't hear.
Then he got in
the truck,
slamming the heavy, rusted

door behind him,
and started the engine
making the muffler
stutter and pop.
As he drove
down the street,
the rumble receded.
The sky was immense,
pale blue
above the Rockies,
and the town
was hard,
lonely,
and still.
I went back to bed,
turned away
from the window
and slept with
no dreams.

Lee Hotel and Gift Shop, Yuma, Arizona

Late at night
in the Lee Hotel
you either leave
on the TV
or take on the dreams
of the people
who've slept there—
a migrant worker
on the night before camp,
your arms turn
to wings
as you circle,
scanning the barren desert
for prey.
A dying old woman
falling suddenly
off a steep cliff
into nothing—
the bottom not bottom
but only more space.
A stranger waking
to dirty walls breathing
and the face in the mirror
is yours but not yours
as the eyes
turn against you
to bleed bitter, red tears.
Then you're slipping and merging
with the body beside you
and you can't even tell
where the boundaries lie
as flesh turns to liquid

still conscious
and everywhere,
soaking the pale green carpet,
puddling in cigarette burns,
seeping into cracks
in the scarred wooden floor.
After this
you can't sleep
and lie sweating
in the mean dark,
listening to a violent cough
in the bathroom next door,
a baby crying downstairs,
the ceiling fan squeaking,
footsteps moving closer
in the hallway.
And somehow
it's like a prayer,
waiting for dawn
to creep in
behind curtains—
a simple cup of coffee,
the tired, decrepit lobby,
your feet on the sidewalk,
things you can see with your eyes.

Where the Buses Used to Leave

"No bumming in this bar"
reads a handwritten sign
under steer horns
in the Yuma Buffet
at the old Greyhound Station
where the buses
don't stop anymore.
"There will be no
guns and knives
brought into this bar"
reads another by the tap
where a Cocopah woman
pours a one-dollar draft
and tells me they have burgers
and bags of Lays chips.

There are no men here
but me,
only stern women
playing pool
or watching news on TV
with no sound.
They do not look at me
and no one speaks English
but the bartender,
to me,
and then only briefly.

The food is bad
but I eat it,
smile,
order more beer,
and listen
to the voices

and the words
I don't know.

After the beer,
I pay and walk out
onto the empty street.
It's a cool, quiet desert night
and a mockingbird is hidden
in a big old elm,
singing
to the waning moon.

Spring Training

Everything recedes
with the dying sun
in my rear-view mirror
as I drive east on 8
over the mountains
into the desert,
losing myself
in AM radio—
the stupid talk shows,
Norteño music,
and yesterday's ball scores.
I speed past farm workers
milking the last few minutes
of twilight
and an overturned car
by the side of the freeway,
surrounded by spectators
and flashing red lights,
a patrolman inspecting
the face smashed
into the windshield.

Like a Warhol death,
I think, and drive faster,
trying to make Yuma
before the first pitch.

Across the Colorado
I exit on 4th Street,
drive past lowriders
bouncing their cars,
the Yuma Cabana Motel,
a dimly lit diner with signs
for pancakes

and Texas-style chili.
I roll down the window
for fresh desert air,
rich with the promise
of Friday night
and it all makes me wish
I could forget and remember
the pastoral dream
of easy belief
and unspoken yearning
in cardboard boxes
full of hotdogs and beer cans,
the living crowd
crammed into the bleachers,
the beautiful symmetry
of the diamond
and fresh green grass.

All the meaningless rituals
that are never enough—
tapping cleats with the bat
between pitches,
stepping out of the box,
trying to decipher the signs.

This Much I Know About Desire

Before I die I just want the life of
    a minor league ballplayer,
        riding the bus to forgotten small towns,
        feeling the bat handle,
        taking the count pitch by pitch.
    The Zen Buddhist Monk,
        rising in darkness to sit in full lotus,
        do daily chores,
        and sound the big bell at the first light of dawn.
    The jazzman playing hole-in-the-wall clubs for too little money,
        smoking in alleyways,
        losing himself in the sudden sweetness of moments
        made new in old tunes.
    The nameless man in a bar by a rooming house,
        having a morning beer
        before dreaming and drifting
        alone through the streets of the unexplored city.
    The underdog candidate in a race for Congress,
        reading the faces,
        feeling the pulse of the crowd
        as she stands up to speak,
        painting a picture of a populist century
        where people not profits
        are the measure of justice.
    The cook in a Mexican restaurant
        where families swear by her thick corn tortillas,
        mole poblano
        and salsa made fresh every day.
    The small farmer who still owns his land
        and works it with passion
        and love for the soil,
        cursing the banks
        as he chats by the fence
        with his neighbor,

the red sky blazing beyond
the shadow
of oaks
in the distance.
The woman who never got married
but loved many men
with her heart and her soul,
and thinks of them fondly
as she writes her last novel
in a house by
the ocean.
The grandfather of many children
who hugs them and tells them
of the strikes in the '30s
where they shut down the factories
and sang songs in the house
of their misery.
The exiled traveler
in a room in Oaxaca
not reading the news
of American nonsense
but waiting for the Day of the Dead.
And after these, just a taste of a day as
an artist at work in his studio, lost in the texture of
paints.
A craftsman who carves wood with the hands of a master
and knows the history
of objects.
A woman who knows the names of the birds—the skylark,
the night heron,
the Japanese white-eye.
A gardener who transforms her yard
to a paradise
drowning in daffodils
and big bulbous red peonies.
A photographer who captures the faces of sorrow,
freezing the beauty of tragedy.
A hospice worker who cares for the dying,
bearing witness
as they learn

how to pass.
A teacher who, in a moment of insight,
sees how little
he actually knows.
A petty criminal who outwits the police.
A cop who outsmarts a corrupt corporate lawyer.
Someone who knows how to follow an animal,
not for the hunt
but for the wonder
of seeing.
And although it's a lot to ask, perhaps just an hour
setting the anchor,
smelling the sea air,
waiting for
the first fish
to bite.
Driving through desert as the sun fades to evening,
feeling alone in the world.
Walking through city streets, watching strangers,
and loving the dance
at the height of the day.
Reading the paper in a neighborhood diner,
eavesdropping whenever I can.
Listening to music in a foreign tongue,
not knowing
what anything means.
Losing myself in a junk shop, sifting through
placemats and old magazines,
before finding a diary by a sad little girl
who must have been
dead now for 25 years.
Watching basketball in a dank city gym,
smelling the sweat,
hearing the squeaking shoes
on the hardwood,
the bounce of the ball
on the timeworn floor.
Riding a freight train on the way to Montana,
drinking tequila with a menacing stranger,
speaking of places to hide.

Climbing the ruins at the foot of the mountain,
nursing the mystery of stones.
Gazing in silence at the altar of skulls
in a Medieval church in Prague.
Making love in a strange room so long and intensely
that it feels like a trading of souls.
And then maybe a minute more
To ponder the nature of non-being.
To remember vision through the eyes of a child.
To hear deeply into music, then sound.
To feel the rough edges of things.
To give in to anger and yield to forgiveness.
To see myself through the eyes of a stranger.
To just be.
To pray without praying.
To dream a whole life in a minute.
To awaken to the rebirth of desire.
And finally, just a second more
Of diving deeply into the texture of things—air,
earth, water, fire, objects made and worn by
hands.
Of holding myself on the edge of abandon.
Of swimming in the center of delight.
Of the spark of passion in beautiful eyes.
Of the warm touch of skin—lips, nipples, stomachs,
thighs.
Of a slant of ethereal light.
Of the smell and taste of the first bite of an apple.
Of seeing the crowd as a family of being—feeling
connected to the bodies and minds of a myriad
of strangers.
Of sudden and welcome revelation.
Of finding myself by losing myself.
Of looking long out my window at the skyline at night
wondering and yearning for what
I don't know.
All of these lives, days, hours, moments and more
I desire
and adore.

Acknowledgments

I would like to thank my first editor in chief, Kelly Mayhew, for her thorough evaluation and editing of this text. My eternal gratitude is also extended to Alys Masek, Hector Martinez, and Manuel Paul López for their painstaking edits and evaluation of the book. Much appreciation to Perry Vasquez for the cover design and Will Dalrymple for the layout. And thank you to Manuel Paul López, Chris Baron, and Kendra Tanacea for their wonderful blurbs.

"Our Lady of Fatima Shrine, Wailua, Maui" first appeared in *California Quarterly*.

A shorter version of "Learning to Be No One" first appeared in column form in *Words and Deeds*.

An earlier version of the poem "Molokai" was first published in *City Works*.

"Naked," "Into the Bardo," "Stars," "What Was it Like?" and "This One Small Life" appeared in my poetry collection *Into the Bardo* on Kelsay Books.

An earlier version of "Bombay Beach, CA" was published in *Cedar Hill Review* and appeared as part of a column in *Words and Deeds*.

Earlier versions of "A Mile Before Mecca" and "Processional" were published in *City Works*.

An earlier version of "Blues" was published in *Portfolio* magazine.

"Costs" was first published in *Cedar Hill Review*.

"Asbestos" was first published in *We Accept Donations* and then *Pacific Review*.

"The Pantry" was first published in *The Moment*.

"Work" was originally published in *Portfolio* magazine and appeared in my first novel, *Drift*, on University of Oklahoma Press.

An earlier version of "L.A." was published in *Pacific Review*.

"Volunteers" was first published in *Pacific Review*.

"Toledo, Ohio, USA" was a finalist for the Allen Ginsberg Poetry Award and was initially published in *Patterson Literary Review*.

A portion of "This Much I Know About Desire" was published as part of *Drift* on University of Oklahoma Press.

About the Author

Jim Miller is a native San Diegan and a graduate of the MFA program at San Diego State University. In addition to his MFA in Fiction, he has a PhD in American Culture Studies from Bowling Green State University in Ohio. He teaches English, Humanities and Labor Studies at San Diego City College and lives in San Diego with his wife, Kelly Mayhew, and son, Walter.

Miller is the author of the poetry collection *Into the Bardo* (Kelsay Books, 2024), and his novels include *Last Days in Ocean Beach* (SD City Works Press, 2018), *Flash* (AK Press, 2010), and *Drift* (University of Oklahoma Press, 2007 and 2024). He is also co-author of a history of San Diego, *Under the Perfect Sun: The San Diego Tourists Never See* (with Mike Davis and Kelly Mayhew on The New Press, 2003 and 2005) and a cultural studies book on working-class sports fandom, *Better to Reign in Hell: Inside the Raiders Fan Empire* (with Kelly Mayhew on The New Press, 2005). In addition to this he is the editor of *Sunshine/Noir: Writing From San Diego and Tijuana* (City Works Press, 2005), *Sunshine/Noir II: Writing From San Diego and Tijuana* (with Kelly Mayhew on City Works Press, 2015), and *Democracy in Education; Education for Democracy* (AFT 1931, 2007). He has published poetry, fiction, and non-fiction in a wide range of journals and other publications, and, along with Kelly Mayhew and Doug Porter, has a Substack journal called *The Jumping-Off Place* as well as a weekly column in the blog *Words and Deeds*, a monthly column in the *San Diego Union-Tribune's* "Community Voices Project," and he previously wrote for the *San Diego Free Press* and the *OB Rag*.